MYSTERIES UNWRAPPED:
THE REAL MONSTERS

WRITTEN BY
SUDIPTA BARDHAN-QUALLEN

ILLUSTRATED BY
JOSH COCHRAN

STERLING

New York / London
www.sterlingpublishing.com/kids

Library of Congress Cataloging-in-Publication Data Available

10 9 8 7 6 5 4 3 2 1

Published by Sterling Publishing Co., Inc.
387 Park Avenue South, New York, NY 10016

Text © 2008 by Sudipta Bardhan-Quallen
Illustrations © 2008 by Josh Cochran
Distributed in Canada by Sterling Publishing
c/o Canadian Manda Group, 165 Dufferin Street
Toronto, Ontario, Canada M6K 3H6
Distributed in the United Kingdom by GMC Distribution Services
Castle Place, 166 High Street, Lewes, East Sussex, England BN7 1XU
Distributed in Australia by Capricorn Link (Australia) Pty. Ltd.
P.O. Box 704, Windsor, NSW 2756, Australia

Printed in China

Sterling ISBN 978-1-4027-3776-3

Book design by Joshua Moore of beardandglasses.com

For information about custom editions, special sales, premium and
corporate purchases, please contact Sterling Special Sales
Department at 800-805-5489 or specialsales@sterlingpublishing.com.

"HE WHO FIGHTS WITH MONSTERS MIGHT TAKE CARE LEST HE THEREBY BECOME A MONSTER."
—FRIEDRICH NIETZSCHE

CONTENTS

They're everywhere. In movies, on TV, in books—even in our minds. As much as we may believe that there is a rational explanation for the bump in the middle of the night, the dark shapes in the closet, the rustling noise under the bed, we are still scared that there is something out there ready to eat us. When we hear a scary sound or catch a glimpse of a shadowy form, we are likely to suspect a monster more than a tree branch brushing up against a window. So…are monsters real?

Every society since the dawn of time has told tales of unknown and frightening monsters. Ghost stories have been told since before there was paper to write them on. Many of the monsters we're afraid of today have been part of human mythology for hundreds, or thousands, of years.

Over time, scientific inquiry has shed light on these monsters in the dark. Almost every monster myth can be traced back to some kind of explanation. There are medical reasons for some legends and psychological reasons for others. Some myths originated from unexplained discoveries, while others were born in the imagination of individual people. But does that mean that monsters aren't real—or might they be?

1. THE CURSE OF THE MUMMY

In 1922, Egyptologist Howard Carter conducted an archaeological dig in Egypt sponsored by Lord Carnarvon. He uncovered the tomb of the pharaoh Tutankhamun, known as "King Tut." By the time the tomb was opened and entered on February 17, 1923, the discovery created a great deal of excitement—the tomb had lain nearly undisturbed for more than 3,000 years and was filled with all sorts of treasure. When Carter entered the tomb, he found incredible sights. Inside King Tut's sarcophagus was a gilded wooden coffin, which in turn housed two more coffins. The third and final coffin was entirely made of gold and held King Tut's mummified remains, untouched since it was buried.

Carnarvon and Carter were instant celebrities. But as the work started on cataloging and examining Tut's tomb and contents, mysterious things began to happen. Carnarvon, who had been among the first to enter the tomb, was bitten on the cheek by a mosquito. The bite quickly became infected, and he died within a week. The "curse" of the mummy was born, with newspapers around the globe reporting that a supernatural force was behind Carnarvon's death. Some even cited an ancient Egyptian inscription in association with the curse: "Death shall come on swift wings to him that toucheth the tomb of Pharaoh."

To add to the superstition, strange details were reported. For example, on the day that Tut's tomb was opened, Carter's pet canary was eaten by a cobra, an animal that symbolized the ancient pharaohs. At the moment that Carnarvon died, the lights across Cairo went out for five minutes. In addition, at this same moment at two o'clock in the morning, Carnarvon's dog, Susie, howled and dropped dead back in England. Many people believed in the curse of the mummy, and soon, the curse had become an accepted part of Tut's legend.

MENACING MUMMIES

Long before the discovery of King Tut's tomb, people have been fascinated by mummies. Some of the first people to express fear of mummies were the Arabs, who conquered Egypt in A.D. 641. The Arabs believed that Egyptians practiced magic during their funerals. They saw evidence of this in the paintings on the walls of Egyptian tombs, which suggested that mummies could return to life—perhaps to seek revenge against trespassers.

In fact, the word "mummy" comes from the Persian word *m?miya*, which means bitumen, a dark, heavy oil. Because the skin of unwrapped mummies was often blackened, the Persians thought that bitumen was used on the bodies. This misconception persisted long enough for the name to stick.

In the 1700s and 1800s, Europeans began to think of mummies as things to be feared. Many stories arose about mummies who were undead creatures and could rise up again to terrorize the living. In 1827, a science fiction novel called *The Mummy* was written by Jane Webb Loudon. Its plot centered on a vengeful mummy who comes back to life and threatens to strangle the book's hero. Later, in 1869, Louisa May Alcott wrote a short story called *Lost in a Pyramid; or, The Mummy's Curse*. The appearance of curses in mummy myths only intensified people's fear of mummies.

WHAT ARE MUMMIES?

In Egyptian history, mummies were not creatures of evil. Rather, the ancient Egyptians mummified their dead relatives to make sure their loved ones' souls would reach the next life. According to Egyptians, the soul needed to recognize the body in the afterlife so that it would have a place to live. Therefore, the body had to be preserved through mummification.

The process that the Egyptians used to mummify the dead changed over time. The first mummies were "accidental"—the bodies were buried in the sand of the desert. Natural conditions dried out the bodies and preserved them. Later, the Egyptians developed a complicated ritual for mummification that tied in with their religious beliefs.

The exact formula for mummy-making, or embalming, evolved and could even vary from mummy-maker to mummy-maker. Between about 2660 B.C. and 2200 B.C., mummy-making involved winding sixteen layers of linen around the body. Plaster was applied to the linen bandages to create sort of a sculpture. The face of the deceased person was painted onto the plaster-covered linen. During this time, mummy-makers sometimes removed the internal organs and packed the abdomen of the body with linen. Around 2200 B.C., plaster was sometimes replaced by resin, and the face of the mummy was painted green, the color of resurrection. These early mummies were not well-preserved—moisture remained in the bodies, so the tissue rotted beneath the bandages,

By 2100 B.C., most mummies had their internal organs removed, except for the heart, which was almost always left inside the body. Instead of painting on a face, the Egyptians began to place a funerary mask over the mummy's head. Within a few hundred years, the brain was also removed before mummification by carefully inserting special hooked instruments up through the nostrils to pull out bits of brain tissue.

Mummy-making reached its pinnacle around 1060 B.C., when mummies were made as lifelike as possible. Internal organs were removed through an incision in the abdomen, wrapped, treated, and returned to the body. The bodies were then dried with natron, a type of salt with great drying properties. Additional natron packets were placed inside the body. To make the mummy appear more realistic, sunken areas of the body were filled with linen, sawdust, sand, and mud, and fake eyes, made from stone, glass, or painted linen, were added. Traditionally, male bodies were painted red, whereas female bodies were painted yellow.

The next step was the wrapping. Hundreds of yards of linen bandages, weighing over twenty pounds, were needed for every mummy. Often, fingers and toes were wrapped individually before the entire hand or foot was wrapped. After the funerary mask was in place over the face and resin was applied between layers of bandages, the final linen strips were wound, and the mummy was complete.

King Tut's funerary mask, as shown in this photograph, was made of gold adorned with semi-precious stones and glass. The mask is housed at the Egyptian Museum in Cairo, Egypt, along with other artifacts from King Tut's tomb. (COURTESY LIBRARY OF CONGRESS)

THE TRUTH BEHIND THE CURSE

Mummification was a regular part of the Egyptians' religious rituals. While the soul lived on, there was no indication that the Egyptians believed that the body became reanimated. Furthermore, though it may have been considered sacrilegious to disturb a mummy, there is no historical evidence that the Egyptians cursed the tombs of mummies.

King Tut's curse was apparently created by media hysteria. Many of the reported examples of the curse were later shown to be exaggerations or distortions of the truth. Despite the prediction that death will come on "swift wings" to those who entered Tut's tomb, of the twenty-two people there when the sarcophagus was opened, only two had died with ten years—hardly a swift death. Furthermore, the inscription itself is a myth—it has never been found in Tut's tomb or among the artifacts. Carter's canary was never eaten by a cobra—it was given in good health to a bank manager. The lights in Cairo did not go out at the moment of Carnarvon's death—however, around the time of his death, the lights in the hospital did go out, but the lights in Cairo are notorious for going out, even today. Finally, though no one knows for sure whether Carnarvon's dog died at the same moment he did, it seems highly unlikely, especially since England and Cairo are in different time zones. Two o'clock in the morning in Cairo is not two o'clock in the morning in England.

TOMB TOXINS

Still, as late as the twenty-first century, people could not fully explain why Lord Carnarvon died so suddenly and mysteriously, from something as apparently harmless as a mosquito bite. In 2005, however, scientists offered a new possible explanation for Carnarvon's death.

As Jennifer Wegner, an Egyptologist at the University of Pennsylvania Museum in Philadelphia, explained: "When you think of Egyptian tombs, you have not only dead bodies but foodstuffs—meats, vegetables, and fruits [provided for the mummy's trip to the afterlife]. It certainly may have attracted insects, molds, [bacteria], and those kinds of things." The molds and bacteria, in particular, could be very toxic to humans.

At least two potentially dangerous types of mold (*Aspergillus niger* and *Aspergillus flavus*) have been found on Egyptian mummies. These molds can cause symptoms ranging from congestion to bleeding in the lungs. In addition, bacteria like *Pseudomonas* and *Staphylococcus* have been found on tomb walls—both of these organisms can cause respiratory problems.

Of course, Carnarvon died long after his exposure to Tut's tomb—so it is unlikely that tomb toxins alone caused his death. Furthermore, the other people who entered the tomb with Carnarvon did not suffer from the same mysterious ailment. In that sense, Tut's curse is still unexplained.

This photograph shows twentieth-century mummies on display at a Mexican cemetery in the city of Guanajuato. These bodies were mummified naturally. The arid climate dried out the skin and tissue before it had time to decompose. (© GEORGE PICKOW / GETTY IMAGES)

MORE THAN ONE WAY TO MAKE A MUMMY

Egypt was not the only place to find a mummy—they have also been found in places such as Northern Europe, South America, Japan, Greenland, Mexico, Lebanon, the Philippines, Russia, and Australia. The ancient Egyptians weren't even the first people to mummify their dead—the Chinchorros people from South America may well have been the first. They preserved their dead from around 5000 B.C.—two millennia before the Egyptians began experimenting with mummification.

The Chinchorros used a very different procedure to make mummies than the Egyptians. Between 5000 B.C. and 3000 B.C., the Chinchorros people dismantled the bodies, treated them, and then put them back together. They removed the arms, legs, head, and skin from the body, and then all the individual parts were heat-dried to strip all the tissue from the bone. The skull was cut in half at the eyeball level to remove the brain. Afterwards, the skull was dried and tied back together. The body was packed with feathers and clay, and the limbs and spine were strengthened by sticks placed under the skin. Finally, the skull was reattached to the body.

Next, the body was covered with a white ash paste. This paste was used to fill out the normal facial features. The skin was then refitted onto the body and painted with a chemical called manganese. The manganese gave the mummies a black color, which is why these are known as "black mummies."

Later on, between 2500 B.C. and 2000 B.C., the Chinchorros made mummies using a totally different method, creating "red mummies." The body was not disassembled; instead, cuts were made to remove the internal organs and to dry the torso. The head was still cut off and then reattached after the brain was removed, but the skin was usually not replaced. On top of the reattached head, the Chinchorros added a wig made from tassels of human hair—some pieces up to two feet long—held in place by a clay "hat" of sorts. The mummy was then painted with red ochre.

2. VAMPIRES: BLOODSUCKERS OF THE NIGHT

In 1732, an investigator named Johannes Fluckinger was sent to the village of Medvegia, in Serbia, to look into the case of a possible vampire. A former soldier named Arnold Paole had recently died after breaking his neck in a fall from a wagon. Local legend had it that Paole had had some kind of a run-in with a vampire near Gossowa in Turkish Serbia. After the encounter, Paole had smeared himself with the vampire's blood in order to free himself from the vampire's curse. By all accounts, that did not work, and Paole became a vampire.

After Paole's death, villagers began to complain that Paole had come back from the dead to attack living human beings and cattle. Four people were said to be his victims within a month of his death. When Paole's body was dug up forty days after burial, it was discovered that his remains had not decayed and that fresh blood flowed from his eyes, nose, mouth, and ears. The villagers decided that Paole was a true vampire and drove a stake through his heart. This action caused Paole to groan aloud and begin to bleed.

Since it was proven that Paole was a vampire, the villagers felt that his victims would also turn out to be vampires. They began to open all suspicious graves to examine the bodies. They found several troubling things.

The body of a twenty-year-old woman named Stana, which had been buried for two months, was found to be undecayed. Her internal organs were well preserved, and her arteries were filled with fresh blood. The body of a sixty-year-old woman named Miliza, who was thought to have eaten the meat from animals that had been attacked by vampires, was found similarly preserved. She had been quite thin while she had been alive, but witnesses remarked that she appeared plumper in death and that her body was full of liquid blood.

Several other bodies were found to be undecayed and full of fresh blood. Fluckinger also reported that, when he dissected the body of a twenty-year-old woman named Stanoika, he had found a bloodshot blue mark, as long as a finger, under her right ear. Since Stanoika died of an illness, it was not clear what made the mark.

Fluckinger and the villagers collected the undecayed bodies and cut off their heads. The remains were burned, and the ashes thrown into the river. Word of the incident, however, spread across Europe. Similar vampire attacks—and subsequent unearthing of suspected vampires—were reported for decades.

VAMPIRISM SPREADS ACROSS THE GLOBE

Vampire legends exist throughout the world, from ancient Babylon and Egypt, Europe, and Asia. Hollywood and literature have created an image of the vampire—with bloodless skin, sharp fangs, an Eastern European accent, and coffin-shaped sleeping arrangements—that does not always fit with the traditional tales. One of the most common themes in vampire tales involves a grave opening in the dead of night, with something unnatural and eerie escaping. It is a vampire, back from the dead, looking for new victims. The vampire will spread illness and death, often beginning by attacking the members of its former family before moving on to feed on its neighbors and friends. Throughout history, however, everything from how a person became a vampire to what form a vampire could take changed from one legend to the next.

From ancient times, people have feared bloodsucking monsters. In Babylon, female demons called the "Lilu" would roam the earth in the hours of darkness to hunt and kill newborn babies and pregnant women. These creatures are said to have craved those victims' blood. The richest source of vampire legends is from the Slavic people of Eastern Europe—especially Russia, Bulgaria, Serbia, and Poland.

The Slavic people believed in several causes for vampirism. A person who was born with teeth, a tail, or a caul (a thin, shimmery, filmy coating that can partly cover a newborn's head and face immediately after birth) was fated to become a vampire. Also, people who were conceived on certain unlucky days, who died strange deaths, who were excommunicated, or who were buried without the proper burial rituals became vampires.

To prevent a person from becoming a vampire, Slavic people would place a crucifix inside the coffin, drive thorns or stakes through the body into the ground below to pin it down, or place blocks under the person's chin to prevent him from opening his

WHEN PAOLE'S BODY WAS DUG UP FORTY DAYS AFTER BURIAL, IT WAS DISCOVERED THAT HIS REMAINS HAD NOT DECAYED AND THAT FRESH BLOOD FLOWED FROM HIS EYES, NOSE, MOUTH, AND EARS. THE VILLAGERS DECIDED THAT PAOLE WAS A TRUE VAMPIRE AND DROVE A STAKE THROUGH HIS HEART.

mouth and eating the funeral shroud. Some people would even bury a potential vampire with a scythe, a farm tool that has a curved blade, positioned over the neck. The scythe's blade was long and sharp, so when the vampire rose from the dead, it would decapitate itself on the cutting edge. To destroy a vampire, the body could be staked, decapitated, or burned or the grave could be sprinkled with holy water and the funeral service could be repeated.

Vampires were also common in nearby Romania. These creatures shared a number of characteristics of the Slavic vampires, with slight differences. The Romanians believed in many of the same causes of vampirism as the Slavs, but they also believed that the seventh son or daughter in a family would become a vampire, as would people who died before baptism, the children of pregnant women who did not eat salt, and people who were bitten by vampires during life.

Several traditions arose among Romanians about how people could detect or kill vampires. Garlic was a potent anti-vampire agent. In fact, living vampires were sometimes "detected" by passing out garlic in church and identifying who did not eat it. As with other legends, a vampire could be destroyed by driving a stake through its heart and then cutting off its head. Garlic was sometimes placed in the mouth of the decapitated head to further hurt the vampire. In extreme cases, the vampire's body was dismembered, and the pieces were burned.

This movie still from the 1931 film *Dracula* shows the title character with his next victim. Actor Bela Lugosi played Count Dracula and helped create an image of vampires that is still popular today. (© UNDERWOOD & UNDERWOOD/CORBIS)

UNDEAD BLOOD DRINKERS

Across cultures, the most common legends about vampires stemmed from the fact that these creatures were "undead"— neither dead nor alive—and that they drank the blood of their victims. They are usually linked to some supernatural phenomenon—since, after all, the dead do not come back to life under normal circumstances.

In reality, there is no scientific evidence to support the existence of the vampires seen in legends. There are, however, a number of medical conditions that create symptoms similar to vampire characteristics. For example, while the fresh growth of fingernails and hair was thought to be proof of vampirism, the truth is that after death, skin recedes and can give the appearance of growth. Also, gases in the body expand and cause the stomach to appear bloated—even though the corpse hasn't been feasting on blood. Many people think that misinterpreting these medical symptoms may have created vampire legends in the first place.

One popular explanation for vampirism is a rare disease called "porphyria." People with porphyria have an imbalance in a blood pigment called "heme," which can lead to mouths and teeth that appear reddish. A severe case of porphyria could make the person highly sensitive to sunlight—in some people, even a mild sun exposure could cause scars to appear on the face, the nose and fingers to fall off, and the lips and gums to become so taut that the teeth project like fangs. People like this would avoid sunlight and become nocturnal. Porphyria sufferers also experience psychiatric problems and may have dementia.

There have been reports that people with porphyria tried to treat their symptoms by drinking human blood in an effort to replace the heme that they were missing. This would tie in with the vampire myth—except that there is no evidence to suggest that drinking blood would help the symptoms at all, or that porphyria sufferers would have even known enough about the cause of their illness to try to drink blood. Also, anything in blood that could help porphyria symptoms would not survive the digestive process.

Another explanation for vampirism could be the disease rabies. About two hundred years ago in Eastern Europe, vampire myths were rampant. Around the same time, there was a rabies epidemic raging. Some symptoms of rabies include appetite loss, fatigue, fever, a colorless complexion, and vomiting blood, and exposure to sunlight can trigger violent outbursts. A person infected with rabies will often attack and bite people.

Perhaps the most likely physical cause for the origins of the vampire myth is a condition called "catalepsy." During a cataleptic episode, the person's body freezes. His muscles become stiff and rigid, and his heart rate and breathing slow. The episode could last many hours or even days. The person could easily be mistaken for a corpse, especially hundreds of years ago when the condition was not well understood.

If a person was buried during a cataleptic episode, he would most certainly try to escape the coffin when he regained his senses. He would perhaps even try to return home. Since catalepsy often occurs in people with schizophrenia, epilepsy, or some other disorder, it is possible that the person not only would "return from the dead" but would exhibit strange behavior as well.

AN ETERNAL MYSTERY

We will never know what exactly inspired the original vampire myths. The likelihood is that the myths arose from psychological fears instead of medical misunderstandings. And despite any explanations that could be uncovered, vampires, and the fears they represent, are likely to haunt us for a long time—at least in our imaginations.

VAMPIRES AMONG US

Though most people now believe that vampires are imaginary, there are still pockets of the world where the legends live on and are taken seriously. In 2003, in Malawi, hundreds of protesters dragged a government official from his house and stoned him after accusing him of harboring vampires. There was a widespread belief that the nation's government was conspiring with vampires to collect human blood in exchange for international food aid.

Furthermore, in 2006, a self-proclaimed vampire declared himself a candidate for governor of Minnesota. The candidate, Jonathon "The Impaler" Sharkey, said, "Politics is a cut-throat business"—which would seem to be perfect for a vampire.

3. COUNT DRACULA: VAMPIRE PRINCE

As we burst into the room, the Count turned his face, and the hellish look that I had heard described seemed to leap into it. His eyes flamed red with devilish passion. The great nostrils of the white aquiline nose opened wide and quivered at the edge, and the white sharp teeth, behind the full lips of the blood dripping mouth, clamped together like those of a wild beast.With a wrench, which threw his victim back upon the bed as though hurled from a height, he turned and sprang at us.

—From *Dracula*, by Bram Stoker

The most famous vampire in the history of the world—Count Dracula—has inspired fear and terror for over a century. Writer Bram Stoker created this gruesome vampire in his 1897 novel, *Dracula*, and the character has become a permanent part of popular culture. Every Halloween, several Count Draculas make appearances at parties and go out trick-or-treating. The general image of Dracula—fangs, slicked back hair, and a cape—can be found on everything from television shows to breakfast cereal.

Interestingly, many people believe that Stoker based his fictional vampire on a real person—the terrifying and formidable Vlad epe. Vlad was a fifteenth-century ruler of Wallachia, a region of the Balkans in present-day Romania. The word *epe* means "impaler"—which translates to one of Vlad's nicknames,

"Vlad the Impaler." Vlad was also known by another name—Vlad Dracula. Though Vlad was no sweetheart, he was definitely not a vampire in the traditional sense—he was not undead, and he didn't feast on blood. Still, there was plenty to inspire a legend.

THE SKINNY ON VLAD

Vlad the Impaler was a brutal ruler. He had to fight for his throne, which may have made him somewhat vicious—although, by all accounts, Vlad was pretty vicious to begin with. As a youth, his favorite pastime seemed to be capturing birds and mice in order to torture and mutilate them. He beheaded some, or he tarred-and-feathered them before setting them free. Most of Vlad's captives were impaled on tiny spears.

Later, as ruler of Wallachia, Vlad tortured and executed many people in the same way that he had done with animals. Everyone—women or children, high-born lords or peasants, foreigners or Vlad's own subjects—risked facing Vlad's wrath. Many people believed that Vlad enjoyed these executions.

Vlad employed an impressive list of torture techniques during his reign. He drove nails into his victim's heads, cut off their limbs, noses, or ears, blinded them, strangled them, skinned them, or burned them alive. Vlad's favorite method of torture, however, was impaling his victim on a stake.

Normally, Vlad attached a horse to each of his victim's legs while the sharpened stake was forced into the body. The stake was never too sharp, to make sure the victim did not die too quickly. He would order thousands of people to be impaled at a single time. In 1459, Vlad had 30,000 people from the Transylvanian city of Brasov impaled; a year later, it was 10,000

EVERYONE—WOMEN OR CHILDREN, HIGH-BORN LORDS OR PEASANTS, FOREIGNERS OR VLAD'S OWN SUBJECTS—RISKED FACING VLAD'S WRATH.

in Sibiu. People estimate that Vlad may have had approximately 100,000 people killed in this way during his reign.

THE BIRTH OF DRACULA

Word of Vlad's brutality may have made an impression on Bram Stoker. Though Vlad was never accused in his own time of being a vampire, his thirst for blood made him a good candidate for a bit of slander. In fact, in Vlad's lifetime, German pamphlets were published to stir up opposition. These pamphlets often had titles like "The Frightening and Truly Extraordinary Story of a Wicked Blood-Drinking Tyrant Called Prince Dracula" and were sometimes illustrated with dark portraits of the man and his atrocities. Despite these claims, there's no evidence that Vlad himself ever drank blood.

There are a number of reasons to think that Vlad the Impaler was the basis for Stoker's Count Dracula. First of all, the two share the same name—Dracula. Since the name "Dracula" was not particularly common, it seems likely that Stoker drew some inspiration from the original Dracula. In fact, Stoker was originally going to call his character "Count Wampyr," but changed his mind when he learned that the word "Dracula" was related to the Romanian word for devil.

In addition, Stoker's novel contains some details that mirror Vlad's real life. Dracula's physical description is very similar to historical accounts of Vlad's appearance. The fact that Dracula is repulsed by Christian objects like a crucifix and holy water may relate to the fact that Vlad had renounced the Orthodox Church in his lifetime. Vlad's first wife had killed herself upon hearing from her husband's enemies that Vlad was dead—even though the news was a trick. The Church refused her a Christian burial because of the suicide, and with that, Vlad had had enough of the Church. Records indicate that Vlad drew a sword, stabbed a crucifix, and said, "I will live my life for blood because the blood is the life." (Of course, quotes like this didn't help the vampire reputation at all.)

CONTRADICTING EVIDENCE

There are, however, many people who believe that Vlad had nothing to do with Count Dracula, except perhaps to give Stoker a better name than "Wampyr." Elizabeth Miller, a professor at Memorial University of Newfoundland, is among those people who argue that there is no real connection between the character Dracula and the historical Vlad. She argues that Stoker had already created his vampire character before he came across any reference to Vlad, so there was no way he could have based Dracula on Vlad. In addition, Miller argues that Stoker didn't seem to know very much about Vlad beyond his nickname of "Dracula"—after all, if Stoker had known about the impalings, those details would have made sense to add to his horror novel.

DRACULA'S LEGACY

Regardless of the true inspiration, Count Dracula and Vlad the Impaler have been permanently connected in most people's minds. But while the rest of the world remembers Vlad as a bloodthirsty monster, in his home of Romania, Vlad is remembered quite differently. Says Miller, "if you go into the big museum in

Although most of the world remembers Vlad the Impaler as a vicious man, Romanians honor him with statues such as this one, which stands in Tirgoviste Park in Wallachia, Romania. (© Simon Marsden / Getty Images)

Bucharest, the National History Museum, there's a room there dedicated to Vlad, and his bust is in the foyer. And there are statues of him and streets named after him in two or three Romanian cities ... And in some parts of Romania, for example, up near his fortress, he's very well remembered. The local people still tell legends about the wonderful things he did. He's looked upon as a sort of Robin Hood character ... When Romanians say 'Dracula,' they are usually thinking about Vlad. They're not thinking about vampires."

HOW DRACULA GOT HIS NAME

Vlad the Impaler got his now-famous nickname through heredity, although there is some disagreement about the details of the story. In one account, Vlad's dad, an earlier Vlad, had been a part of the Romanian *Order of the Dragon*. In Romanian, "the dragon" is *dracul*— so the older Vlad became known as Vlad Dracul ("Vlad the Dragon"). Since the Romanian ending *ulea* means "the son of," Vlad the Impaler was also called "Vlad Dracula."

However, there's another translation of the Romanian word *dracul*—it can also mean "devil." This makes young Vlad "the son of the devil"—and implies that Vlad the Impaler's mean streak may have run in the family. (Dad must have had some kind of temper to earn the nickname of "devil.")

4. WEREWOLVES: SHIFTING SHAPES

According to a centuries-old historical pamphlet, in 1590, people in the town of Bedburg, Germany, lived in mortal fear of wolves. Wolf attacks were so frequent that people were reluctant to travel from one town to another. Every morning, people would rise to the sight of human casualties.

The townspeople tried to kill the wolves in the surrounding areas, but nothing stopped the attacks. One day, a group of people hunting with dogs, sharp sticks, and spears cornered a particularly vicious wolf. While they attacked, the wolf—instead of running away—stood on its hind legs and transformed into a middle-aged man. The townspeople recognized him as Peter Stubbe, a local man.

As Stubbe was tortured, he provided the townspeople with a strange confession. He claimed to have begun practicing sorcery at the age of twelve and had made a pact with the Devil in exchange for a magic belt. When Stubbe wore the belt, he could take the form of a wolf—according to the pamphlet, in fact, "a greedy, devouring wolf, strong and mighty, with eyes great and large, which in the night sparkled like unto brands of fire, a mouth great and wide, with most sharp and cruel teeth, a huge body and mighty paws." In this form, he could attack anything or anyone he wanted. Stubbe bit into his victims' throats and drank their blood.

In his so-called confession, Stubbe claimed that he would frequently attack the young girls out milking cows in the fields. Once, he said that he attacked a group of three people, two men and a woman. These people wandered close to the forest where Stubbe hid out. They heard someone calling to them and went to explore, one by one. Later, the mangled corpses of the two men were found by neighbors—but the woman's body was never recovered. It was thought that Stubbe devoured her whole—there was nothing left for others to find.

Following his confession, Stubbe was executed and decapitated. His body was burned to ashes. As word of his trial and punishment spread, people began to believe that others like Stubbe—who had the power to transform into wolves to commit heinous acts—were living among them. In this way, the legend of werewolves was born.

A LEGENDARY BEAST

Like vampire stories, werewolf legends are found all over the world. In ancient Greece, there was a story about a vicious king named Lycaon who was transformed into a wolf by Zeus, king of the gods. In Norse mythology, werewolf legends may have originated with the warriors known as berserkers. Berserkers dressed themselves in wolf or bear hides and fought so ferociously that onlookers thought they were immune to pain.

Historically, there were a number of ways that a person could transform into a werewolf. Like Peter Stubbe, anyone could wear a wolf belt, usually made from wolf skin, to transform into a wolf. Usually, an actual physical transformation was not required—most werewolf legends describe a divided self, in

Throughout history people have feared deadly wolf attacks. This wood engraving from 1859 accompanies a story about a heroic ax-wielding wife who saves her husband from a wolf. (COURTESY LIBRARY OF CONGRESS)

which the human body was found curled up asleep either in bed or under a bush in the woods while the werewolf incarnation was on the prowl. In other cases, the wolf shape was worn like clothing over the human body. Sometimes, werewolves only partially transformed—a medieval account of a werewolf attack left by a victim named Benoist Bidel describes the werewolf as having forefeet that looked like a man's hands.

Many werewolf legends involve transformations during a full moon, but this wasn't the only time that humans could change into werewolves. Many legends state that a person could swallow an enchanted drink or rub a magical ointment on the body to transform into a werewolf. One Russian legend said that to become a werewolf, a person had to jump over a fallen tree in the forest and then stab it with a small copper knife while chanting a spell. In some cases, drinking the water out of a werewolf's footprint or being bit by a werewolf was enough to make someone into a werewolf as well.

Werewolves could return to human form in several ways. Some could transform back at will. Others had to simply remove their wolf belts to become human again. Many traditions suggest that the werewolf must bathe in running water to return to normal.

POSSIBLE EXPLANATIONS

Since werewolf legends are so common throughout the world, over the years, there have been several attempts to explain their origin. One recent theory has to do with food poisoning. There were many reports of werewolves in Europe in the eighteenth and nineteenth centuries. In that time, it is possible that entire towns ingested "ergot," a fungus that grows on rye during wet spring seasons that follow cold winters. Chemicals in ergot are similar to those found in the drug LSD, and ergot poisoning causes paranoia, hallucinations, and mass hysteria, as well as twitches, convulsions, and spasms. Some people believe that the hallucinations from ergot poisoning could explain why some individuals believed that they were werewolves, and that the mass hysteria could explain why entire towns believed that they had seen a werewolf. Unfortunately, there is no way to prove for sure that ergot poisoning was the cause of werewolf legends.

Other explanations for werewolf legends are similar to the explanations for vampirism. Rabies and porphyria are cited as possible causes for these myths because of the violent behavior or physical disfigurement that these conditions cause. However, these ailments do not explain the wolf-like appearance that werewolves supposedly take on.

A condition called "hypertrichosis" might be a good explanation for werewolf stories. Those who have this condition have an excessive amount of hair growing on their faces and bodies. Hypertrichosis is sometimes called "Human Werewolf Syndrome" because people affected by this condition resemble wolves or dogs due to the excess hair. However, hypertrichosis is an extremely rare disease—it occurs in only 1 out of 10 billion people. There are only ninteen documented cases of hypertrichosis in the world today, and seventeen of those cases are in the same family. The rarity of the condition makes it difficult to believe that hypertrichosis is the only basis for werewolf myths.

This c.1880s portrait shows Mat Me, a Burmese woman afflicted with hypertrichosis. Symptomatic of hypertrichosis, her face is covered with hair. This condition may have given rise to werewolf lore and is sometimes called "werewolf syndrome." (© BETTMANN/CORBIS)

STILL FEARSOME

Werewolf stories continue to circulate and scare people, even in modern times. Despite everything we know about werewolves and various theories about the legends, sometimes something mysterious happens, and the existence of werewolves seems to be all too possible.

In 1790, in North Wales, a stagecoach was attacked and over-turned by a gigantic beast almost as long as the coach horses. A year later, a nearby farmer saw enormous wolf-like tracks in a snow-covered field. He followed the tracks for two miles and found a lake of blood with scattered carcasses of livestock all around. He then saw a huge black animal that looked like a wolf ripping the throat out of his dog. The farmer barricaded himself into his house, but the wolf followed. The animal then stood up on its hind legs like a human and looked through the windows of the house before running off into the night.

Two centuries later, in 1992, an enormous animal was once again spotted in Wales—this time, by the light of a full moon. The sighting happened just before a farmer discovered two of his lambs had been slaughtered. Many people believed the animal was a Welsh werewolf—but we will never know for sure.

HOW TO KILL A WEREWOLF

According to legend, there are several ways to kill a werewolf. Piercing the werewolf's body with silver, shooting it with a silver bullet, or stabbing it with a silver-tipped spear—which is considered one of the best ways to kill a werewolf. Supposedly, if the werewolf is pierced near the heart, it is very likely it will implode, leaving behind either a dazed and confused shapeshifter or empty air.

5. THE LIVING DEAD: ZOMBIES

This is the way Zombies are spoken of: They are the bodies without souls. The living dead. Once they were dead, and after that they were called back to life again. No one can stay in Haiti long without hearing Zombies mentioned in one way or another, and the fear of this thing and all that it means seeps over the country like a ground current of cold air. This fear is real and deep.

—From *Tell My Horse*, by Zora Neale Hurston

In Haitian culture, references to zombies are extremely common, and they relate to important aspects of a Haitian religion. Many Haitian people historically practiced a religion called voodoo. Voodoo is rooted in West African traditions, and voodoo practitioners believe in the spirit world and magic spells. Voodoo sorcerers, called *bokor*, were thought to be able to use magic to bring dead bodies back to life as zombies. The *bokor* would capture the victim's *ti bon ange*, a part of the soul, in the process of creating a zombie.

Usually, the person who would become a zombie had done something to make his relatives or neighbors angry with him. They would then hire a *bokor* to turn him into a zombie. Zora Neale Hurston described the process in her book, *Tell My Horse*: "After the proper ceremony, the Bocor in his most powerful and dreaded aspect mounts a horse with his face toward the horse's tail and rides after dark to the house of the victim. There he places his lips to the crack of the door and sucks out the soul of the victim and rides off in all speed. Soon the victim falls ill, usually beginning with a headache, and in a few hours is dead."

Voodoo believers dance, sing, and make offerings to the voodoo spirit. This ca. 2005 photograph shows believers dancing in the Souvenance temple in Haiti after sacrificing a goat. (© SAUL SCHWARTZ/GETTY IMAGES)

Once brought back to life, the zombie was essentially a mindless slave to the *bokor* who called him back. Legend has it that the zombie would work tirelessly at any task given to him, even the grueling work on a Haitian plantation. The zombie would remain mindless in this way until the *bokor* died.

The *bokor* kept the victim's *ti bon ange* in a closed container to maintain control of the zombie. The only things that could break the zombie's trance were breaking the container to free his *ti bon ange*, the death of the *bokor*, and eating salt. When a zombie was fed salt, he would turn on the *bokor* and attack him, or would return to his burial site and try to dig his way in—typically dying in the process.

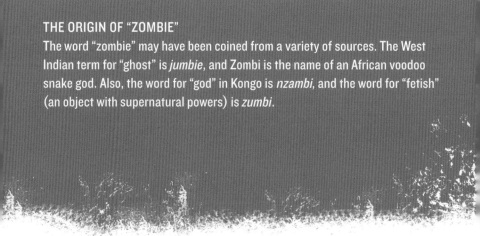

THE ORIGIN OF "ZOMBIE"

The word "zombie" may have been coined from a variety of sources. The West Indian term for "ghost" is *jumbie*, and Zombi is the name of an African voodoo snake god. Also, the word for "god" in Kongo is *nzambi*, and the word for "fetish" (an object with supernatural powers) is *zumbi*.

THE CASE OF CLAIRVIUS NARCISSE

Several zombie stories have been recorded over the years. In 1980, a man who claimed to be Clairvius Narcisse appeared in a rural village in Haiti. He stumbled across a woman he said was his sister in a marketplace. The original Clairvius Narcisse, though, was thought to have died on May 2, 1962—eighteen years earlier. But the newcomer was able to answer questions about his childhood and family that no one else could have known. Narcisse said that he had been presumed dead, but he was merely paralyzed and still conscious. He even claimed to remember the doctor covering his face with a sheet.

Narcisse then claimed that he had been resurrected by a *bokor* and made into a zombie. Further questioning and research into Narcisse's past revealed that he had been sold to a *bokor* by his brothers because he refused to sell his share of the family's land. After the *bokor* had unburied him, he sent Narcisse to work as a zombie slave on a sugar plantation with many other zombies. The *bokor* died in 1964, but Narcisse wandered around Haiti for the next sixteen years in a haze.

Narcisse's story began a scientific inquiry into Haitian zombies. His original death was documented in a hospital, so many people believed that he really could be a zombie—and that studying what happened to him might reveal some truths about zombies.

SCIENTIFIC ANSWERS

Dr. Wade Davis was one of the people studying Narcisse's case. He learned that a *bokor* would use complex formulas, called "zombie powders," during the zombie-making rituals. Dr. Davis found out that, often, there were four ingredients common to the zombie powders: puffer fish, which often contain a deadly poison called "tetrodotoxin"; a marine toad, *Bufo marinus*, which also produces toxic substances; a tree frog, *Osteopilus dominicensis*, which produces a substance that can irritate the skin; and human remains. In addition, the zombie powders also contained other things that would inflame the skin, like ground-up lizards or spiders or even ground glass.

Dr. Davis thought it was very interesting that puffer fish—and therefore, tetrodotoxin—were used to make zombies. Tetrodotoxin poisoning causes paralysis and sometimes death. People poisoned by tetrodotoxin often stay conscious while paralyzed, and some appear dead but eventually recover. Dr. Davis noticed that Narcisse's description of being paralyzed but conscious could be explained by tetrodotoxin poisoning.

Dr. Davis formed a theory—that when zombie powder was applied to a victim's skin, the irritating ingredients like ground glass would cause breaks in the skin. The poisons like tetrodotoxin could pass into the blood through the breaks in the skin, and the victim then would appear dead. After burial, the *bokor* could remove the victim from the grave, and when the victim regained his senses, he would believe that he was a zombie. Some *bokor* fed zombies a paste that was made from jimson weed, known in Haiti

SHE WAS MUTE AND UNRESPONSIVE, AND WHEN HER TOMB WAS OPENED, IT WAS FOUND TO BE FILLED WITH STONES.

as "zombie's cucumber." This plant causes fever, hallucinations, and amnesia, and these symptoms could make the victim believe that he really had changed into a zombie.

THE FULL EXPLANATION?

Of course, Dr. Davis's theory doesn't fully explain everything about zombies. For one thing, when other scientists tested the zombie powders, they found that some of them contained very little or no tetrodotoxin. This suggests that one poison alone does not create all zombies. In addition, when some of the zombie powders were tested on lab rats, they had no paralyzing effect.

Other researchers, including Dr. Chavannes Douyon and anthropologist Dr. Roland Littlewood, feel that many supposed zombies are actually people who suffer from psychiatric conditions or brain damage. In fact, some researchers have suggested that zombie legends may have arisen in Haiti as a cultural way to explain wandering mentally ill people.

In their research, Drs. Douyon and Littlewood identified three potential zombies and studied them. The first was a thirty-year-old woman who was identified by her family by a scar on her face three years after her burial. She was mute and unresponsive, and when her tomb was opened, it was found to be filled with stones. The family believed that the woman's husband had made her into a zombie—but when she was examined, it was found that she suffered from a psychiatric disease called catatonic schizophrenia.

The second potential zombie was a thirty-one-year-old woman who had been missing for thirteen years. When her family found her, she claimed that she had been kept as a zombie in a village 100 miles away. She did not, however, act like a typical zombie—instead of seeming mindlessly dead, she was talkative and giggled frequently. When doctors examined her, they found that she was not genetically related to the family that had believed her to be their missing loved one, and that she suffered from a variety of mental and developmental symptoms.

In the last case, it was also found that the supposed zombie was not biologically related to the family who reclaimed him. In this case, a twenty-six-year-old man was found over a year after his burial wandering near his hometown. He was mute and did not respond to others. The man's father accused the victim's uncle of zombification and had him arrested, but a medical examination revealed that the man suffered from epilepsy and other mental illnesses.

Many people, in Haiti and other places, still believe in zombies. The religion, voodoo, is also still practiced by many. Though there are several misconceptions about zombies and voodoo, they have become a standard part of horror movies, ghost stories, and legends. Zombies still walk the earth—in our minds and on our television screens.

A BRIEF HISTORY OF VOODOO

The religion called voodoo has been practiced for 6,000 years or more. Some experts believe that more than 60 million people practice voodoo, which means "spirit." It is one of the world's oldest ancestral, nature-honoring traditions.

People who believe in voodoo believe that spirits, or *Loa* run the universe. There are many *Loa* responsible for different parts of the world. During a voodoo ceremony, believers gather outside, and a voodoo priest makes a sacrifice to the *Loa*. Voodoo practitioners believe that the *Loa* give prophecies, advice, or warnings, and people ask the *Loa* for health and happiness.

Sometimes movies and books portray voodoo as a dark and evil religion that is dominated by black magic and pin-stuck voodoo dolls. In reality, these things are not a part of traditional voodoo practices. According to photographer Lynne Warberg, who has documented Haitian voodoo for years, voodoo is like any religion. "Participation in voodoo ritual," she says, "reaffirms one's relationships with ancestors, personal history, community relationships—and the cosmos. Voodoo is a way of life."

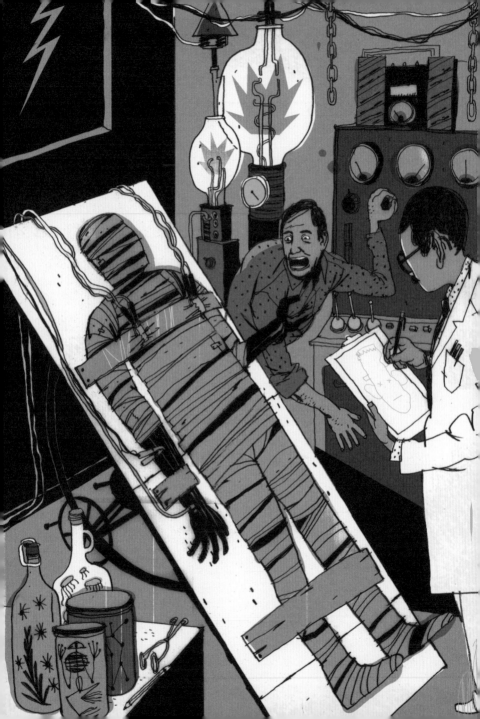

FRANKENSTEIN'S MONSTER:
6. SCIENCE RUN AMOK

His yellow skin scarcely covered the work of muscles and arteries beneath; his hair was of a lustrous black, and flowing; his teeth of a pearly whiteness; but these luxuriances only formed a more horrid contrast with his watery eyes, that seemed almost of the same colour as the dun white sockets in which they were set, his shrivelled complexion and straight black lips.

... I beheld the wretch—the miserable monster whom I had created. He held up the curtain of the bed; and his eyes, if eyes they may be called, were fixed on me. His jaws opened, and he muttered some inarticulate sounds, while a grin wrinkled his cheeks ... I escaped, and rushed down stairs. I took refuge in the courtyard belonging to the house which I inhabited; where I remained during the rest of the night, walking up and down in the greatest agitation, listening attentively, catching and fearing each sound as if it were to announce the approach of the demoniacal corpse to which I had so miserably given life.

—From *Frankenstein*, by Mary Shelley

In 1816, a nineteen-year-old girl named Mary Wollstonecraft Godwin changed the world of monsters forever. That summer, while she was visiting some friends in Geneva, Switzerland, sudden lightning storms prevented Mary from leaving the house she was staying in on the shores of Lake Geneva, the Villa Diodoti, at night. She spent the night at the villa with the poet Percy Bysshe Shelley, who would later become her husband, George Gordon, Lord Byron, and Lord Byron's physician, Dr. John Polidori. To pass the time, the group read a French translation of a collection of German ghost stories, *The Fantasmagoriana*. Soon, they made a pact to see who among them could write the most frightening ghost story.

Inspired by the challenge, Mary had a nightmare about a man who tried to create life out of dead things. She explained, "I saw the pale student of unhallowed arts kneeling beside the thing he had put together. I saw the hideous phantasm of a man stretched out, and then, on the working of some powerful engine, show signs of life, and stir with an uneasy, half vital motion ... [The student] would rush away from his odious handiwork, horror-stricken."

Within a few months, Mary had written an entire novel, and on January 1, 1818, her book, *Frankenstein*, appeared in print—under her married name, Mary Shelley. Since then, there are more than two dozen different editions of the novel in print and several plays and movies have been made based on the novel. Frankenstein's monster is now a standard part of Halloween and horror shows—all because of a nineteen-year-old's imagination.

THE BIRTH OF FRANKENSTEIN

Unlike many monster myths, Frankenstein's monster was not a centuries-old legend. Instead, history knows exactly when and where this monster was born—in the mind of Mary Shelley that

The 1931 movie *Frankenstein* popularized the image of Frankenstein's monster. This still image from the film shows Frankenstein's monster, played by Boris Karloff. (© BETTMAN/CORBIS)

summer in Switzerland. Mary had many sources for inspiration, from her own life and from the scientific breakthroughs that were being made in her day.

In the 1800s, when Mary was writing, physicians were interested in the boundary between life and death. Many experiments were performed to revive people who had just passed away using resuscitation and electricity. In fact, Mary's husband Percy's first wife, Harriet, had drowned in 1816. Rescuers took her lifeless body and tried to revive it using smelling salts, vigorous shaking, electricity, and artificial respiration with bellows. These methods had been used since the 1760s to restore drowning victims to life. Though Harriet did not survive, the episode may have inspired Mary. She was already very interested in the idea of the dead coming back to life, especially after the death of her premature infant daughter. Mary even had a dream in March 1815, that her daughter was held before a fire, rubbed vigorously, and restored to life.

Electricity, in particular, plays a large role in Dr. Frankenstein's experiments. To bring the monster to life, Dr. Frankenstein says, "I collected the instruments of life around me, that I might infuse a spark of being into the lifeless thing that lay at my feet." The "spark" is assumed to be electricity. In the late eighteenth century, a scientist named Luigi Galvani had discovered that the legs of a dead frog could move if he jolted it with a spark of electricity. Mary's understanding of this phenomenon, called "galvanism," was that electricity could somehow release life forces. Conversations that summer on such subjects lead to Mary's wondering, "perhaps a corpse would be re-animated; galvanism had given token of such things."

One of the things that makes Frankenstein's monster particularly repulsive is that he is made of body parts collected from various corpses. In Mary's day and in modern times, decaying tissue and rotting body parts stir disgust in most people, and

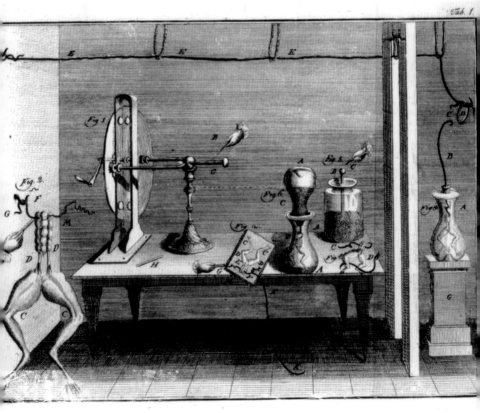

Luigi Galvani's experiments demonstrated that a jolt of electricity could make a dead frog's legs move. These experiments may have contributed to Mary Shelley's conception that electricity could bring a dead person back to life. (COURTESY LIBRARY OF CONGRESS)

there is almost an automatic assumption that someone made from such gruesome parts would be a monster as well.

MAD SCIENCE

Frankenstein has become more than just a novel or a monster—the word itself is a part of modern language. In fact, we now have words such as "frankenfood" (which refers to food that has been genetically modified) and "frankenword" (which refers to a word made from the fusion of two or more other words).

The dictionary definition of the word "Frankenstein" is "an agency or creation that slips from the control of and ultimately destroys its creator"—essentially, Frankenstein has become interchangeable with the idea of science out of control. Frankenstein's monster continues to be scary because people can identify with the fear of the unknown that the monster represents. After all, the more science advances, the more possibilities arise for terrible experiments like Frankenstein to become real.

A MODERN MISUNDERSTANDING

As much as Frankenstein's monster has become a part of modern culture, many people today routinely confuse Frankenstein with the monster. In Mary Shelley's novel, Dr. Frankenstein is the scientist who creates the monster. The monster itself is often referred to as "the creature" or "the fiend," but Mary never gave it a name.

In 1931, Mary's novel was made into a movie called *Frankenstein*, starring Boris Karloff as the monster. Since that movie, the public began to think of the monster as "Frankenstein"—a notion further reinforced by later films such as *Bride of Frankenstein* and *Son of Frankenstein*.

GHOSTS:
7. TRAPPED BETWEEN TWO WORLDS

In June of 1929, the most famous ghost hunter in England, Harry Price, found himself in the middle of a murder mystery at the "most haunted house in England," Borley Rectory. Price was an expert investigator of ghosts and hauntings who had pioneered several scientific approaches for hunting ghosts with cameras, telephones, and forensic techniques. Borley Rectory had been considered a haunted house ever since 1863 when the first disturbances were noticed by the Reverend Henry Bull.

Witnesses and residents complained about strange noises in the night and ghostly apparitions walking through the house and grounds. Some of the ghosts included a girl in white, a headless man, and a nun. Despite the scary sounds and visions, the owners of the house quickly became used to their ghosts. They even built a special porch so they could sit out with cigars after dinner and keep watch for the ghosts.

In 1930, however, the mood in Borley Rectory changed. A new priest and his wife moved in, and the entertaining ghostly behaviors were replaced with breaking windows, moving furniture, and flying objects. The ghosts even physically attacked the new tenants. Strange messages addressed to the priest's wife, Marianne, like "Marianne, please help get" and "Get light mass and prayers here," began appearing on the walls. Eventually, the couple began to believe that one of the ghosts had been a Catholic nun. For years, this haunting went on until Marianne and her husband moved out in 1935—and Price moved in.

Over the next years, Price and his team of researchers—sometimes up to forty of them—searched the house for clues and evidence. They eventually communicated with a ghost named Marie Lairre who claimed to be a former Catholic nun. Marie had left the convent to get married, and the ghost claimed that her husband, Henry Waldegrave, then had murdered her and buried her in the cellar. Shortly after that message, another spirit warned the researchers that the house would be burned to the ground that night and that the evidence of the murder would finally be revealed.

The next morning, though, the house was still standing. A few months later, the researchers called off the search without any further proof of ghosts. The house was sold to Captain W. H. Gregson. While he was moving his possessions into the house, he knocked over an oil lamp in the library. That started a fire, and the rectory was completely gutted—eleven months after the spirit predicted the house would burn down.

In the rubble of the destroyed building, Harry Price found the bones of a young woman. The remains were finally given a proper burial. The mystery of Borley Rectory was solved.

Right: This 1943 photograph shows the ruins of the Borley Rectory shortly after it burned down. The photographer of this image claimed that the white object in the darkened doorway floated up from the ground as he snapped the picture. (© David E. Scherman/Time & Life Picture/Getty Images)

WHERE GHOSTS COME FROM

Ghosts are typically thought of as the disembodied spirits of the dead. They have been a part of mythology and folklore in virtually every society throughout time. Writings from the ancient Babylonian *Epic of Gilgamesh* from around 2000 B.C. are among the earliest recorded references to ghosts: "Enkidu's shadow rose slowly toward the living / and the brothers, tearful and weak, / tried to hug, tried to speak, / tried and failed to do anything but sob."

Although descriptions of ghosts have changed over time, the reasons for ghosts to continue to haunt the Earth have remained largely the same. The first major reason for the birth of a ghost is that a dead body was not buried according to the proper religious rituals. As far back as the ancient Greeks, it was believed that if a body was not properly buried, the soul would be denied entrance to Hades and would be forced to wander forever. It is still often thought that ghosts will appear if someone is buried in ground that was not consecrated to a god or if the grave is disturbed.

The other major source of ghosts is through violent or unfair deaths. It is widely believed that the spirits of people who are murdered continue to haunt the Earth, often at the site of the murder. Many people believe that especially when children die in a house, whether by murder or by accident, their spirit remains.

THE TRUTH BEHIND GHOSTS AND HAUNTED HOUSES

Today, most ghosts are associated with haunted houses. Modern-day versions of Harry Price have investigated these houses and have often come up with different explanations for noises and other ghostly phenomena. Their explanations are based on the similarities between ghost sightings—most ghosts are seen at night in older houses, often on particularly cold nights.

It is not surprising that ghosts are expected in older houses. These houses have seen more history, and, because more people have lived in them, it is more likely that something bad has happened in them. However, it was the fact that most sightings take place on cold nights that led investigators to think about other ways to explain the ghosts.

Because old houses have been around so long, they are often in a bit of disrepair. Floorboards are loose; there are gaps in the outer walls that let breezes in; the windows don't seal properly. As it turns out, these problems in the houses often create the conditions commonly associated with a ghost sighting.

The key to explaining ghostly observations is to understand how things, especially old houses, react to a cold, dark night. At night, the air is cooler than during the day. As a result, parts of the house actually contract, or get smaller—not very much, but just enough to make the creaks louder and the gaps between the house and the outside world larger. When the wind blows, the pressure on the house causes creaks. The cold air that leaks in creates the drafts that are associated with the chill that some people describe feeling when a ghost is near.

ENKIDU'S SHADOW ROSE
SLOWLY TOWARD THE
LIVING / AND THE BROTHERS,
TEARFUL AND WEAK, / TRIED
TO HUG, TRIED TO SPEAK,
TRIED AND FAILED TO DO
ANYTHING BUT SOB.

Cold and damp air is also more dense than warm air, so it carries sounds better. Noises that are far away sound closer; noises anywhere in the house sound like they could be right next to the observer.

Of course, not all ghost sightings take place at night in old houses. There are reported hauntings in all fifty states, in old houses, in new buildings, on battlefields, and even in vineyards. A new generation of ghost hunters is trying to find proof of ghosts using sophisticated equipment that detects small changes in electromagnetic fields or temperature. There's no telling where the next ghost will be discovered.

WILL O' WISPS

"The tricksy lights. Candles of corpses, yes, yes.
Don't you heed them! Don't look! Don't follow them!"
—From *The Two Towers*, by J. R. R. Tolkien

Will o' wisps were a particular kind of ghost. There was nothing cute or friendly about will o' wisps—instead, they were thought to be malevolent spirits that would lead anyone who followed them to their death. In *The Two Towers* Tolkien drew on this myth to add a disturbing atmosphere to a scene in a swamp.

Science has gradually reduced the number of ghosts by explaining the observations as something other than supernatural. In the case of the will o' wisps, it is now commonly believed that they were simply lights seen in swamps that were mistaken for ghosts. The flickering lights were caused by gases such as hydrogen phosphide and methane being released from decaying plants or animals. Since swamps could be treacherous areas and many people did meet their deaths in swamps, the legend of the will o' wisps was born.

8. CYCLOPES: ONE-EYED GIANTS

ODYSSEUS: *Are they hospitable and reverent towards strangers?*
SILENUS: *Strangers, they say, supply the daintiest meat.*
ODYSSEUS: *What, do they delight in killing men and eating them?*
SILENUS: *No one has ever arrived here without being butchered.*
—From *The Cyclops* by Euripides

The ancient Greeks believed that the Cyclopes (a Cyclops is an individual) were a race of fierce one-eyed giants who walked the Earth alongside humans. There are two myths in which Cyclopes are major characters. In the first tale, the three original Cyclopes—Brontes, Steropes, and Arges—were the sons of Gaia, the goddess who represented the Earth, and Uranus, the god who represented the sky. These three Cyclopes forged Zeus's thunderbolt, Poseidon's trident, and Artemis's bow and arrow. Ancient Greeks attributed the noises that came from active volcanoes to the sounds of the Cyclopes working in their workshops creating weapons.

In another myth, the Cyclopes are considerably more ferocious. They lived on an island and were shepherds, raising great herds of sheep and goats. Their culinary tastes, however, were not restricted to livestock—their favorite food was human flesh. According to one story, the legendary Greek hero Odysseus and his men were captured by a Cyclops who ate several of the humans. Odysseus was able to outsmart the Cyclops, blind him, and escape.

CYCLOPEAN WALLS

The legends of the Cyclopes were reinforced by what the Ancient Greeks saw in their towns. In some parts of Greece, such as Tyrins and Mycenae, there are prehistoric structures that were built using unknown techniques. They were built of huge stones and boulders, with very little space between adjacent stones and no mortar between the stones to hold them together. These structures were called "cyclopean walls."

In one structure near Mycenae, one of the stones used above a doorway is estimated to weigh more than 200 tons. Despite this, the cyclopean walls still stand today. When the ancient Greeks discovered these unique structures, they did not believe humans could have built them. One observer, a traveler named Pausanias, wrote of the ruins at Tyrins: "The circuit wall, which is the only remaining ruin, was built by the Cyclopes. It is composed of unwrought stones, each of which is so large that a team of mules cannot even shake the smallest one."

AN EYE ON THE TRUTH

One-eyed beings like the Cyclopes were also found in stories from other parts of the world. In Norse mythology, trolls were often though to be ugly giants who only had one eye. Sedna, the Inuit goddess of the sea, is often depicted as a one-eyed hag. In Sumerian mythology, the demon Humbaba is described as a one-eyed giant with the powers of a storm and breath of fire. Today, Cyclopes still appear as monsters in comic books, video games, and movies.

For the most part, however, the Cyclops was a uniquely Greek monster. The ancient Greeks probably did believe that these creatures existed—after all, only the Cyclopes could have built the massive cyclopean walls. The Greeks probably even felt that they had more powerful scientific proof, given that, when digging in their fields, they found what they thought were "Cyclops bones."

Later, in the fourteenth century, a man named Giovanni Boccaccio made a discovery of ancient bones in Italy. Boccaccio claimed that he had discovered a Cyclops skull inside a Sicilian cave—after all, the skull was much larger than a human skull, and it appeared to have a large eye-shaped hole in the center of its forehead.

Even more recently, scientists excavating in fields on the Greek island of Crete found similar Cyclops-sized bones. But these scientists knew something that Boccaccio or the ancient Greeks did not know—they knew where the bones really came from.

Between 23 and 2 million years ago, a creature called *Deinotherium giganteum* (loosely translated, this means "really huge, terrible beast") roamed parts of Europe. *Deinotherium* was a giant mammal, 15 feet tall with 4.5-foot tusks—and it was a distant relative of the elephant.

While an elephant's trunk—essentially, a stretched-out nose —is pretty hard to miss when looking at a live elephant, it would be almost impossible to guess its existence from looking at a skeleton. The hole that the ancient Greeks thought was for an eye was really the nasal cavity of a long-dead *Deinotherium*. The cavity is very large because there has to be room to accommodate all the muscles of the trunk that need to attach to the skull.

In 1997 Homer's *The Odyssey* was adapted into a two-part television movie. Pictured here is the Cyclops from the movie. (© GETTY IMAGES)

Thomas Strasser, an archaeologist at California State University, Sacramento, says, "The idea that mythology explains the natural world is an old idea. You'll never be able to test the idea in a scientific fashion, but the ancient Greeks were farmers and would certainly come across fossil bones like this and try to explain them. With no concept of evolution, it makes sense that they would reconstruct them in their minds as giants, monsters, sphinxes, and so on." So it would seem that the Cyclops was one creature that really turned out to be entirely a figment of the human imagination.

THE CYCLOPS IN *THE ODYSSEY*

The ancient Greek poet Homer wrote two very famous epic poems, *The Iliad*, which tells the story of the Trojan War, and *The Odyssey*, which recounts the hero Odysseus's journey home after the Trojan War. Odysseus has many adventures along the way, and faces a number of mythical creatures. One of these creatures is the Cyclops: *"Thence we sailed on with aching hearts, and came to the land of the Cyclops, a rude and lawless folk, who, trusting to the immortal gods, plant with their hands no plant, nor ever plough, but all things spring unsown and without ploughing, wheat, barley, and grape-vines with wine in their heavy clusters, for rain from Zeus makes the grape grow. Among this people no assemblies meet; they have no stable laws. They live on the tops of lofty hills in hollow caves; each gives the law to his own wife and children, and for each other they have little care."*

—"*'Polyphemos' from The Odyssey, Book IX*," by Homer
(translation by Richard Hooker)

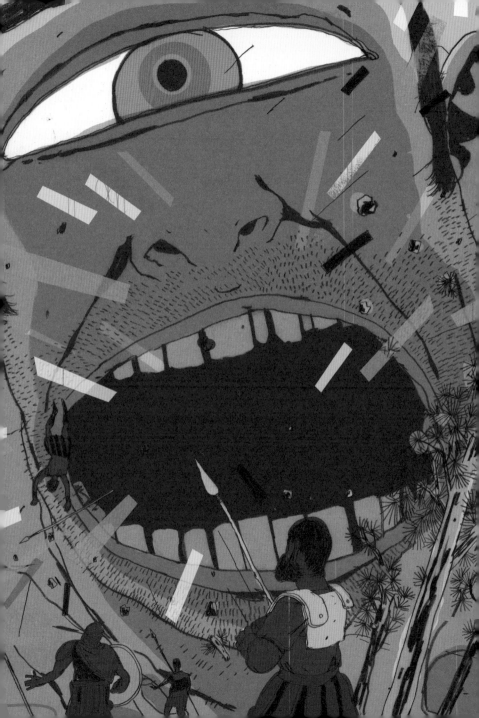

9.

WITCHES: THE DEVIL'S HENCHMEN

On March 18, 1612, in Lancashire, England, a woman named Alizon Device tried to buy some pins from a peddler named John Law. John refused, so Alizon cursed him. Within moments, John collapsed from a seizure.

Alizon was convinced that her curse caused John's seizure, and so she confessed to bewitching him. Witchcraft in 1612, however, carried heavy penalties. Alizon was arrested, and her mother, Elizabeth Device, and her brother, James Device, were also questioned by the magistrate.

Within weeks, the investigation into the witchcraft had expanded. The authorities were no longer interested in just John Law's seizure; instead, they were investigating seventeen suspicious murders. Eventually, thirteen people, known as the "Pendle Witches," were arrested for those murders, including Alizon, Elizabeth, and James. They were all accused of selling their souls to the devil in exchange for the power to kill.

Several of the accused confessed and revealed details of their witchcraft. Elizabeth Device's mother, Elizabeth Southerns, confessed that she made an effigy, or clay symbol, of each of her intended victims and then crumbled or burned the effigies over time. This process caused her victims to sicken and die.

In the end, after the witchcraft trials, eleven of the accused witches were hanged, one died in prison, and one was sentenced to a year in prison. The Lancashire Witch Trials became one of the most famous witch trials in English history.

TRIALS IN SALEM

Another very famous set of witch trials took place in the United States, in Salem, Massachusetts, in 1692. A group of young girls began by accusing three women of bewitching them. The girls went on to accuse several more people of witchcraft, and some of the accused confessed and pointed the finger of guilt at others. The community became hysterical and convicted people of witchcraft based on the flimsiest of evidence. Nineteen people were hanged as witches, one was pressed to death, and at least four, and possibly as many as seventeen, died while in prison before the Salem Witch Trials ended.

There are differences between the Lancashire trials and the Salem trials. In Lancashire, the people who confessed to witchcraft were convicted and put to death. In Salem, on the other hand, people who confessed became prosecution witnesses against other suspected witches and were often spared execution. The Lancashire prosecutions were mostly limited to the people who had attended a meeting at the Devices' family home, Malkin Tower, on Good Friday of 1612—a meeting widely believed to be a Witches Sabbath. The Salem prosecutions were not limited in any sense—everyone from a respected minister, a grandmother, the town beggar, to a Caribbean slave was accused by the girls. No one was safe from prosecution.

As punishment, so-called "witches" in Salem, Massachusetts were sometimes put in a pillory. This 1892 lithograph shows a wooden pillory which locks around a person's neck and wrists—allowing that person to be publicly humiliated and tortured. (COURTESY LIBRARY OF CONGRESS)

IN 1562, IN WIESENSTEIG, GERMANY, A HAILSTORM OCCURRED DURING THE HARVEST SEASON. THE ENTIRE CROP WAS DESTROYED. THE AUTHORITIES ARRESTED SIXTY-TWO WITCHES AND ACCUSED THEM OF CAUSING THE HAIL THROUGH WITCHCRAFT. ALL SIXTY-TWO WERE EXECUTED.

This lithograph from 1892 depicts mayhem at a witch trial in Salem.
(Courtesy Library of Congress)

WITCH HYSTERIA

Throughout much of history, witches have been feared and reviled. The Lancashire and Salem Witch Trials were just two examples of persecutions against witches. Between 1450 and 1750, more than 100,000 people—mostly women, although there were quite a few men—were prosecuted for witchcraft.

Almost anything unlucky or unexplained, such as sudden deaths, crop failures, hailstorms, or famines, was blamed on witchcraft. In 1562, in Wiesensteig, Germany, a hailstorm occurred during the harvest season. The entire crop was destroyed. The authorities arrested sixty-two witches and accused them of causing the hail through witchcraft. All sixty-two were executed. Later, in 1590, after their wedding, King James VI of Scotland and Anne of Denmark encountered a storm on their sea voyage back to Scotland. People believed that witches threw cats into the North Sea and caused the storm to rage. For this inconvenience to King James, a group of people were accused of witchcraft and were arrested and prosecuted.

HOW TO TELL A WITCH WAS A WITCH

As history professor Dr. Brian Levack explains, "The witch was usually not a foreigner or stranger to her community. The great majority of the witches were older and poorer than average, unmarried or widowed, someone who did not adhere to the traditional behavior standards of her community or her sex [meaning that she did not follow society's rules about "a woman's place"], or someone who physically looked different." Though anyone could be accused of witchcraft, there were specific procedures that people followed to prove that a particular person was a witch.

One way to tell who was a witch was to find his or her imp, or familiar. These were demonic spirits who took the form of animals, like cats, dogs, or mice. The imp, or familiar, would help the witch perform dark magic. According to Dr. Levack, "You can imagine in [a] jail in the 16th and 17th century, you're going to get a mouse, all sorts of creatures crawling through there, and the accusers would say 'Oh, there's the imp!' And they would use that as evidence against the witch."

In addition, people would look for a special mark, called the "witch's mark" or the "devil's mark," on the body of a suspected witch. These marks could be any natural physical abnormality, though a devil's mark was generally a scar, birthmark, or skin blemish, while a witch's mark was more often an extra breast (due to a medical condition called "polymastia") or an extra nipple (due to another medical condition called "polythelia").

DISHONEST FACTS

Despite the supposed evidence found against witches, there was a great deal of trickery and fraud involved in witch trials. Often, special examiners were hired to inspect a witch's body for a tell-tale mark. It was believed that the marks could be invisible and could only be discovered by pricking the accused person's body with a needle. The invisible mark would be insensitive to pain and did not bleed. However, the examiners were sometimes known to con people by using blunt needles that caused no pain or bleeding. Furthermore, with modern medical understanding, people now know that some harmless things like warts or corns do not bleed and are insensitive to needle pricks.

Even when accused witches confessed, the confessions were often unreliable. In many cases, people who pled not guilty but were convicted of witchcraft were executed. On the other hand, those who confessed to witchcraft were spared execution—especially if they agreed to testify against other witches.

Confessions were also extracted under horrible conditions. It was not uncommon for witch examiners to use torture on the unlucky suspects. Alleged witches were sometimes deprived of sleep for many nights by being forced to walk the length of their cells until their feet were bloody. Many confessed in a state of total exhaustion, just to be able to get some sleep.

WHITE WITCHES

Long before witches were hunted and feared, in many places, they were considered wise women who used magic for the benefit of humanity. In several ancient religions, women called "white witches" played important roles. With the spread of Christianity, however, pagan beliefs were replaced by the teaching of the Church—and the Church, for the most part, does not acknowledge supernatural power that does not come from their god. At this time, many white witches lost the respect of their communities and became persecuted.

WITCHES TODAY

The world has come a long way from the witch trials of the sixteenth and seventeenth centuries. Being a witch no longer holds the same meaning—in fact, there are many self-proclaimed witches these days. People who practice the nature-worshipping religion Wicca often call themselves witches. They practice the very traditions and even magic spells that centuries ago got people arrested. According to Emory Erickson, cofounder of a Wicca group, "By remaining secretive, many groups foster fear and mistrust in the public. We have no reason to hide in the shadows because we are not doing anything wrong.... It's time to get out of the broom closet we've been in for several hundred years."

Despite all the explanations we've uncovered about the existence of monsters, most people still believe them to be real. Maybe that's because there's always some new piece of "evidence" to open up our minds to interesting possibilities. For example, in June 2007 a tourist claimed to have taken new video of the Loch Ness Monster in Scotland. This footage reignited a decades-old debate about whether the monster was real or an elaborate fake. In Wisconsin, there are stories of the Bray Road Beast, a werewolf-like creature that dozens of people claim to have seen.

There is a lot of scientific proof to explain how monster stories may have begun, but the truth is that there is no way to say that, scientifically, monsters cannot exist. Furthermore, finding explanation for a monster myth does not necessarily mean that all monster legends are untrue. Part of the allure of monsters is that we may never have a full and complete explanation—and so they remain just a little bit scary.

CHAPTER NOTES

The following notes consist of citations to the sources of quoted material. Each citation includes the first and last words or phrases of the quotation and its source. References are to works cited in the Sources, beginning on page 84.

Chapter One: The Curse of the Mummy
PAGE
1 "Death shall ... Pharoah.": Deem
7 "When you ... of things.": Handwerk

Chapter Two: Vampires: Bloodsuckers of the Night
PAGE
19 "Politics is ... business.": Reuters

Chapter Three: Count Dracula: Vampire Prince
PAGE
21 "As we ... at us.": Stoker, p. 336.
25 "I will live ... the life.": Griffith
25-26 "If you go ... about vampires.": FRONTLINE/World

Chapter Four: Werewolves: Shifting Shapes
PAGE
29 "a greedy,... mighty paws.": quoted in Hourihan, p. 122

Chapter Five: The Living Dead: Zombies
PAGE
37 "This is ... and deep.": Hurston, p. 189.
37-38 "After the ... is dead.": Hurston, p. 192.
45 "Participation in ... way of life.": Guynup

Chapter Six: Frankenstein's Monster: Science Run Amok
PAGE
47 "His yellow ... given life.": Shelley, p. 58.
48 "I saw ... horror-stricken.": Shelley, p. 9.
50 "I collected ... my feet.": Shelley, p. 58.
50 "Perhaps a ... such things.": Shelley, p. 8.

Chapter Seven: Ghosts: Trapped Between Two Worlds
PAGE
55 "Marianne, please help get.": Clarke
55-56 "Get light mass and prayers here.": Clarke
58 "Enkidu's shadow ... but sob.": *Epic*, stanza 100
61 "The tricksy ... follow them.": Tolkien, p. 234

Chapter Eight: Cyclopes: One-Eyed Giants
PAGE
63 "ODYSSEUS: Are ... being butchered.": Euripides
64 "The circuit ... smallest one.": Pausanias, 2.25.8
67 "The idea ... so on.": Mayell
67 "Thence we ... little care.": Hooker

Chapter Nine: Witches: The Devil's Henchmen
PAGE
76 "The witch was usually not a foreigner ... or someone who looked physically different.": Levack
77 "You can ... the witch.": Bryant
79 "By remaining ... hundred years.": Crawford

The Last Word
PAGE
81 ... there are stories of the Bray Road Beast: Linda Godfrey; Scarlet Sankey

SOURCES

Belanger, Jeff. *Our Haunted Lives: True Life Ghost Encounters*. The Career Press, Franklin Lakes, NJ, 2006.

Bryant, Michelle. "Witch Trials: Tragic Events Once Led People to Accuse Neighbors of Witchcraft." The University of Texas at Austin, Feature Story, Oct./Nov. 2004. www.utexas.edu/features/archive/2004/witches.html.

Clarke, Andrew. "No Hand Was Visible: The Wall Writings at Borley Rectory." FoxEarth.org, 2003.
http://www.foxearth.org.uk/BorleyRectory/WallWritings.html.

Crawford, Emily. "Out of the Broom Closet." *Albuquerque Journal*. December 23, 2004. Viewed online as "Wiccan Faith Becoming More Exposed as Participation Grows" at
www.rickross.com/reference/wicca/wicca48.html.

Deem, James M. "Egyptian Mummies: Curse of King Tut's Tomb." Mummy Tombs website at www.mummytombs.com/egypt/kingtut.htm.

Epic of Gilgamesh, Tablet XII. www.piney.com/Gil12.html.

Euripides. *The Cyclops*. Trans. E. P. Coleridge. The Internet Classics Archive, http://classics.mit.edu/Euripides/cyclops.html.

FRONTLINE/World. "Interview with the Vampire Queen: Elizabeth Miller." October 2002. www.pbs.org/frontlineworld/stories/romania/miller.html.

Godfrey, Linda. *The Beast of Bray Road: Tailing Wisconsin's Werewolf*. Madison, WI: Prairie Oak Press, 2003.

Greer, John Michael. *Monsters: An Investigator's Guide to Magical Beings*. St. Paul, MN: Llewellyn Publications, 2001.

Griffith, Vivé. "Vampires Never Die." University of Texas at Austin website, Feature Story, Oct/Nov 2003.
www.utexas.edu/features/archive/2003/vampires.html.

Guynup, Sharon. "Haiti: Possessed by Voodoo." *National Geographic News*, July 7, 2004. http://news.nationalgeographic.com/news/2004/07/0707_040707_tvtaboovoodoo.html.

Handwerk, Brian. "Egypt's 'King Tut Curse' Caused by Tomb Toxins?" *National Geographic News*, May 6, 2005.
http://news.nationalgeographic.com/news/2005/05/0506_050506_mummycurse.html.

Hooker, Richard. "Polyphemos from The Odyssey, Book IX." *World Civilizations: Anthology of Readings*, 1996. www.wsu.edu/~dee/WORLD.htm.

Hourihan, Margery. *Deconstructing the Hero: Literary Theory and Children's Literature*. London: Routledge, 1997.

Hurston, Zora Neale. *Tell My Horse*. Philadelphia: J. B. Lippincott Co., 1938.

Levack, Brian. "Witch Trials." University of Texas at Austin, October 25, 2004. http://www.utexas.edu/features/archive/2004/witches.html.

Mayell, Hillary. "Cyclops Myth Spurred by 'One-Eyed' Fossils?" *National Geographic World*, February 5, 2003. http://news.nationalgeographic.com/news/2003/02/0205_030205_cyclops.html.

Oliver, Narelle. *Mermaids Most Amazing*. New York: G.P. Putnam's Sons, 2005.

Pausanias. *Description of Greece*. English Translation by W.H.S. Jones, Litt.D., in 4 volumes. Volume 1. Attica and Corinth. Cambridge, MA: Harvard University Press; London: William Heinemann Ltd., 1918. Internet Ancient History Sourcebook.
www.fordham.edu/halsall/ancient/pausanias-bk2.html.

Reuters. "Vampire Goes for Governor." Carried by ABC News Online, January 13, 2006. www.abc.net.au/news/newsitems/200601/s1547002.htm.

Sankey, Scarlet. "Bray Road Beast: Wisconsin's Werewolf," *Strange Magazine*, No. 10, 1992.

Shelley, Mary Wollstonecraft. *Frankenstein. Frankenstein or the Modern Prometheus; Edited with an Introduction and Notes by Maurice Hindle*, Rev. Ed. London/New York: Penguin Books, 2003.

Stoker, Bram. *Dracula*. New York: Pocket Books, 2003.

Tolkien, J.R.R. *The Two Towers*. Boston: Houghton Mifflin Co., 1954 (1982).

Untermeyer, Louis. *Heinrich Heine: Paradox and Poet (the Poems)*. New York: Harcourt, Brace, and Company, 1937.

Wolf, Leonard. *Dracula: The Connoisseur's Guide*. New York, Broadway Books, 1997.

INDEX